Alaska

Jim Ollhoff

Visit us at
www.abdopublishing.com

Published by ABDO Publishing Company, 8000 West 78th Street, Suite 310, Edina, Minnesota 55439 USA. Copyright ©2010 by Abdo Consulting Group, Inc. International copyrights reserved in all countries. No part of this book may be reproduced in any form without written permission from the publisher. The Checkerboard Library™ is a trademark and logo of ABDO Publishing Company.

Printed in the United States.

Editor: John Hamilton
Graphic Design: Sue Hamilton
Cover Illustration: Neil Klinepier
Cover Photo: iStock Photo
Interior Photo Credits: Alamy, Alaska Aces, Alaska State Library, Alaska Wild, AP Images, Comstock, Corbis, Getty, iStock Photo, Library of Congress, Mile High Maps, Mineral Information Institute, Mountain High Maps, North Wind Picture Archives, One Mile Up, Peter Arnold Inc., Trans Alaska Pipeline, University of Alaska-Fairbanks
Statistics: State population statistics taken from 2008 U.S. Census Bureau estimates. City and town population statistics taken from July 1, 2007, U.S. Census Bureau estimates. Land and water area statistics taken from 2000 Census, U.S. Census Bureau.

Manufactured with paper containing at least 10% post-consumer waste

Library of Congress Cataloging-in-Publication Data

Ollhoff, Jim, 1959-
  Alaska / Jim Ollhoff.
    p. cm. -- (The United States)
  Includes index.
  ISBN 978-1-60453-637-9
  1. Alaska--Juvenile literature. I. Title.

  F904.3.O44 2010
  979.8--dc22
                        2008050999

Table of Contents

The Last Frontier

There is something for everyone in Alaska. There are volcanoes, cliffs, valleys, glaciers, lakes, and tundra. Parts of Alaska are permanently frozen. Other parts get rain on more than half the days of the year.

Alaska is more than twice as big as any other state. It has the highest point in the United States. Alaska has the most lakes, the most wetlands, the most shoreline, and the most wilderness of any state. It also has a low population density. Low density means that it's a huge state, but only 686,293 people live in Alaska.

The word "Alaska" comes from the word *Alaxsxa* or *Alaxsxix*. This is the language of the Aleuts, one of the native Alaskan peoples. The word means either "mainland" or "where the sea breaks its back."

Alaska has the most
wilderness of any state.

Quick Facts

Name: Alaxsxa or Alaxsxix, from the native Alaskan Aluet people, both meaning "mainland" or "where the sea breaks its back."

State Capital: Juneau, population 30,690

Date of Statehood: January 3, 1959 (49th state)

Population: 686,293 (47th-most populous state)

Area (Total Land and Water): 663,267 square miles (1,717,854 sq km), the largest state

Largest City: Anchorage, population 279,671

Nicknames: The Last Frontier, The Great Land, Land of the Midnight Sun, Seward's Folly, Seward's Icebox

Motto: North to the Future

State Bird: Willow Ptarmigan

State Song: "Alaska's Flag"

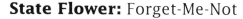

Forget-Me-Nots

State Flower: Forget-Me-Not

State Mineral: Gold

State Tree: Sitka Spruce

Highest Point: Mount McKinley (Denali), 20,320 feet (6,194 m)

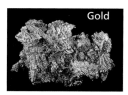
Gold

Lowest Point: Pacific Ocean, 0 feet (0 m)

Average July Temperature: 45° to 72°F (7° to 22°C)

Record High Temperature: 100°F (38°C), in Fort Yukon on June 27, 1915

Sitka Spruce

Average January Temperature: 20° to -20°F (-7° to -29°C)

Record Low Temperature: -80°F (-62°C), in Prospect Creek on January 23, 1971

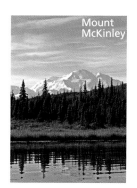
Mount McKinley

Average Annual Precipitation: 10 inches (25 cm) in the north, to more than 200 inches (508 cm) in the southeast

Number of U.S. Senators: 2

Number of U.S. Representatives: 1

U.S. Postal Service Abbreviation: AK

Geography

Alaska's size is 663,267 square miles (1,717,854 sq km). It is by far the largest state in the United States. It has more than 6,600 miles (10,622 km) of coastline facing the Arctic Ocean, the Pacific Ocean, and the Gulf of Alaska.

In the north there are massive areas of frozen ground called permafrost. Ice fields are large areas of ice that form from constant snow and melting over several years. Ice fields cover about 29,000 square miles (72,110 sq km) of the state.

When ice fields meet and pool together, glaciers form. Glaciers become giant masses of ice. There are 100,000 glaciers in Alaska. The largest glacier is the Bering Glacier, covering 2,250 square miles (5,827 sq km).

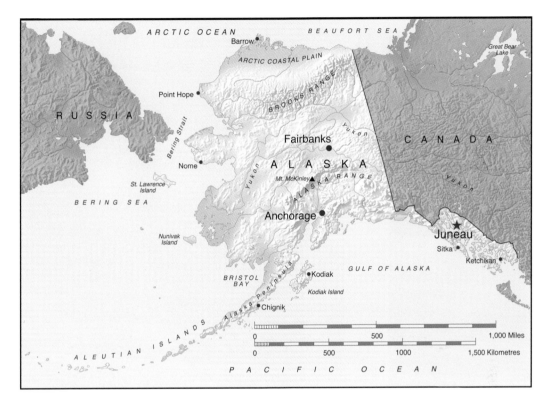

Alaska's total land and water area is 663,267 square miles (1,717,854 sq km). It is by far the largest state. The state capital is Juneau.

Mount McKinley is the highest mountain in North America. Some people travel to Alaska to try to climb it.

Alaska has 39 mountain ranges. Mount McKinley is the highest mountain in North America. It is in Alaska's Denali National Park and is 20,320 feet (6,194 m) high.

There are more than 3 million lakes and 3,000 rivers in Alaska. The longest river is the Yukon, with 1,875 miles (3,018 km) in Alaska alone. The Yukon is the third-longest river in the United States (behind the Mississippi and the Missouri Rivers).

The southwest part of the state is called the Aleutian region. It includes the narrow Alaska Peninsula. Extending out from the Peninsula are more than 69 islands in a trail that projects southwest into the Pacific Ocean. The Aleutian region has many active volcanoes and ice-covered mountains.

The narrow southeast strip of land that borders British Columbia, Canada, is sometimes called the Panhandle. It includes more than 1,000 islands. There are 60 glaciers in the higher elevations.

A glacier in Alaska's Tracy Arm Fjord releases a huge chunk of ice.

Climate and Weather

In Alaska's far north, the average winter temperatures usually range from -5 to -20 degrees Fahrenheit (-21° to -29°C). There's very little rain in the far north, often less than 5 inches (13 cm) per year. The summer temperature gets up to about 55 degrees Fahrenheit (13°C).

The southeast Panhandle area is similar to the northwest coast of the United States. Rain and snow fall at a rate of about 60 inches (152 cm) per year. Winters and summers are milder.

In the middle of Alaska, summer temperatures can go from 45 degrees Fahrenheit (7°C) to 75 degrees Fahrenheit (24°C). Winter temperatures go from 20 degrees Fahrenheit (-7°C) to -10 degrees Fahrenheit (-23°C).

Temperatures vary a lot in different parts of the huge state of Alaska. In general, summers are mild with lots of sunshine. Winters are snowy and bitterly cold.

Plants and Animals

In the north and west of Alaska, the land is an Arctic tundra—a treeless, frozen ground. The tundra has small plants, such as mosses, lichens, herbs, and shrubs.

In the vast interior of the state, there are forests of spruce, birch, aspen, and cottonwood trees. Shrubs are everywhere, such as willow, cranberry, alder, Labrador tea, and blueberry.

In the south, the most common trees are Sitka spruce and other kinds of evergreens. There are many dolphins, sea lions, and sea otters in the waters.

Cranberries, blueberries, lichen, and moss are found in Alaska.

Sea lions rest on a buoy in Prince William Sound, Alaska.

Bald eagles are a common sight in Alaska.

Alaskan parks and wilderness areas are filled with all kinds of animals. Brown bears, black bears, caribou, lynx, mountain goats, and moose are common. More than 40,000 bald eagles reside in Alaska.

In the Arctic areas, about 20 percent of the world's polar bears are found, although their habitat in Alaska is decreasing. Beluga whales, bowhead whales, and orcas are found in the Arctic Ocean and Bering Strait areas.

Wolves are found all over Alaska. Moose are common also, even sometimes walking down city streets. When people look around, they're never sure what animal they'll see next.

A moose stands on a home's front steps.

Grizzly Bear

Mountain Goat

Lynx

History

The first people in Alaska came from Siberia at least 15,000 years ago, and probably much further back. Those immigrants became the ancestors of many of the Native American tribes in North and South America. Through the centuries, many waves of people came into Alaska.

A native Alaskan carries his kayak.

Early in the 1700s, Danish explorer Vitus Bering sailed along the coast of Alaska. He found huge numbers of sea otters. Their furs were very valuable. Russian merchants began to make trips to Alaska, gathering sea otter fur.

A sea otter.

In 1784, Russian traders settled on Kodiak Island. In the following years, Great Britain, Russia, and the United States all tried to gain control of the Alaska fur trade.

The Europeans, with more advanced weapons, killed many native Alaskans. A few of the native Alaskan tribes were able to live peaceably with the European settlers.

Many native Alaskans were killed by the more advanced weapons of the early European settlers.

However, the majority of the natives suffered. Almost 80 percent of the Aleuts were wiped out by violence and European diseases. Most of the Alaskan natives were pushed off their ancestral ground. Some were enslaved and many killed.

In the 1860s, Russia began to lose interest in Alaska. Russia needed money, and the fur trade was declining. Russia began talking about selling Alaska to the United States.

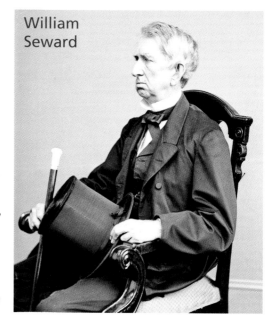

William Seward

In 1867, Secretary of State William Seward authorized the purchase of Alaska for $7.2 million. Many people thought there was little of value in Alaska. Newspapers called it "Seward's Icebox" and "Seward's Folly." But in the city of Sitka, on October 18, 1867, the Russian flag was lowered, and the United States flag was raised.

Salmon canneries were built in 1878. These canneries eventually became the largest in the world.

Gold was discovered in the Canadian Klondike in 1897. For three years, the Klondike gold rush brought thousands of treasure hunters to Alaska. They took boats to cities like Skagway, Alaska, to start their journey into Canada.

Thousands of gold miners trudge up the snow-covered Chilkoot Pass near Skagway, Alaska, in 1898. The pass was the main route to the goldfields.

Americans slowly became aware of the value of Alaska. In the early 1900s, industry leaders began to take advantage of Alaska's resources in minerals, fish, and timber. Fishermen sought whale, salmon, and other fish.

Some experts felt that Alaska would be a good place to defend America. During World War II, the United States Congress approved the rapid construction of military bases and highways in Alaska. Alaskans benefited greatly from these construction projects.

Alaska's Governor Stepovich stands between President Eisenhower and Secretary of the Interior Fred Seaton on July 1, 1958.

It was clear that Alaska was important for military reasons. On January 3, 1959, Alaska officially became the 49th state.

In 1968, huge deposits of oil were discovered on the North Slope, near the Arctic Ocean. In 1977, oil companies finished building the Trans Alaska Pipeline. The pipeline brought many resources into the Alaska economy.

A section of the Trans Alaska Pipeline.

Did You Know?

In 1925, an outbreak of diphtheria occurred in the city of Nome. Diphtheria is a disease of the lungs. It was often fatal in those days. A serum was available that could save those infected, but Nome had none of the medicine. An urgent telegram went out, asking for serum to prevent many deaths. Airplanes couldn't fly in Alaska at that time. So, beginning January 27, 20 teams of dogs and mushers raced toward Nome carrying the serum. They traveled 674 miles (1,085 km) through mountains, shifting ice, blizzards, and freezing temperatures, often with no light.

Many of the mushers endured frostbite. At times, the windchill was -70 degrees Fahrenheit (-57°C). On February 1, the serum arrived safely. While the death toll in Nome was between five and seven, it could have been in the hundreds had it not been for the brave mushers and their hardy dogs.

Each year, the Iditarod Trail Sled Dog Race is held. It is a 1,150 mile (1,851 km) trail from Anchorage to Nome. It reminds people of the brave 1925 serum run.

The Iditarod

The Iditarod Trail Sled Dog Race is 1,150 miles (1,851 km) from Anchorage to Nome.

People

Sarah Palin (1964-) was born in Idaho, but her family moved to Alaska when she was only three months old. She grew up in the town of Wasilla and graduated from high school there. She worked as a reporter, businesswoman, and mayor. In 2006, she made history by becoming the first woman and youngest governor of Alaska. She again made history in 2008, becoming the first woman to run as a Republican vice presidential candidate, sharing the ticket with Senator John McCain.

Vitus Bering (1681-1741) was asked by Tsar Peter of Russia to find out whether Asia and North America were connected by land. In 1728, Bering sailed between the continents and through the water passage that would later bear his name, the Bering Strait. The two continents did not connect. In a second trip in 1741, he and his crew were the first known Europeans to set foot in Alaska.

Benny Benson (1913-1972) was born in Chignik, Alaska. When Benny was 13 years old, he entered and won a contest to design the state flag. His simple design showed the stars of the Big Dipper pointing to the North Star. Alaska adopted his flag in 1927. Later, it became the official flag when Alaska became a state.

Howard Rock (1911-1976) was born in the village of Tikigaq, about 50 miles (80 km) south of Barrow. He was raised as an Inupiat native. He became a spokesman for the native peoples of Alaska. He helped with land claim struggles. He helped to prevent nuclear tests in a harbor near his village. In 1962 he founded the *Tundra Times*, a newspaper dedicated to news and opinion of native Alaskans. He was voted Alaska Man of the Year in 1974, and was nominated for a Pulitzer Prize in 1975.

Libby Riddles (1956-) was born in Madison, Wisconsin. In 1985, she became the first woman to win the Iditarod Trail Sled Dog Race. The Iditarod is an annual 1,150 mile (1,851 km) race from Anchorage to Nome. It helps people remember the 1925 sled dog run that brought life-saving medicine to Nome. In

1985, Libby took just over 18 days to finish the race. She lives in Alaska, and is a sought-after speaker, author, and sled-dog trainer.

Cities

Anchorage, Alaska

Anchorage is the largest city in Alaska. It has a population of 279,671. About half of Alaska's total population lives in and around Anchorage.

Anchorage started as a tent city. It was home to construction workers building the Alaska Railroad from 1915 to 1922. When the work was done, the city stayed.

City Of Tents Anchorage Alaska

Alaska railroad workers.

In June, Anchorage has more than 19 hours of sunlight each day. In December, it has less than six hours of sunlight a day.

Juneau is the capital of Alaska. It has a population of 30,690. The only way to get to Juneau is by boat or airplane. There are no roads into Juneau.

Juneau, Alaska

The Tlingit Indians had been living in the area for thousands of years. However, the city got its name from a gold prospector named Joe Juneau. He laid out plans for a town in 1880. It became a mining camp. Not long after that, the camp became a town.

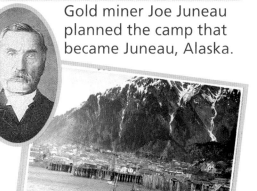

Gold miner Joe Juneau planned the camp that became Juneau, Alaska.

Fairbanks is the largest city in the interior of Alaska. Including the area surrounding the city, Fairbanks has a population of about 87,000. This makes Fairbanks the second largest city in the state.

The city began as a trading post in the early 1900s. Gold prospectors found a place to stay, and bought supplies there. With the coming of highways and railroads, Fairbanks grew to be an activity center for the interior of Alaska.

It can get very cold in Fairbanks. The sign says -52°F (-47°C).

Noon in Barrow, Alaska, in December. The sun doesn't rise from November 18 until January 23.

Barrow is the northernmost city in the United States. The population is 3,982, with another 2,400 living nearby.

The town was formerly known as Ukpiagvik, which means "the place where owls are hunted." The town got its current name from Sir John Barrow, the British navy officer who explored and mapped the Arctic coastline in 1825.

When the sun rises on May 10, it doesn't set again until August 2. That's 54 days of 24-hour sunshine. When the sun sets on November 18, it doesn't rise again until January 23. That's 67 days of night!

Transportation

Railroads began in Alaska as early as 1902. At first, many companies went bankrupt. The first reliable railroad transportation began in the early 1920s. A railway between Anchorage and Fairbanks was one of the first in the state. There are currently about 500 miles (805 km) of rails in Alaska. The longest connects Seward, Anchorage, and Fairbanks. Many railroads only run in the summer.

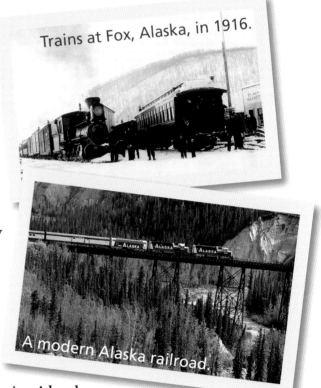

Trains at Fox, Alaska, in 1916.

A modern Alaska railroad.

One of the problems in Alaska is the high cost of transporting goods and products. Roads link the main population centers, but many small villages are only accessible by air. Even Juneau, the state capital, is only accessible by boat or airplane.

Because of the remote locations of many villages, air travel is important. There are more than 800 airfields in Alaska. Most villages have a pilot. Several airlines fly into Alaska.

Travel by boat is also common. There is a ferry system. It is called the Alaska Marine Highway.

Ferries carry cars and people on the Alaska Marine Highway.

Natural Resources

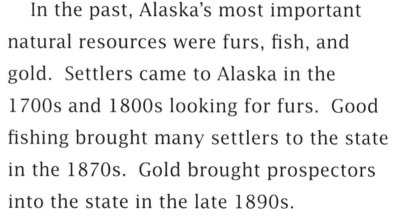

In the past, Alaska's most important natural resources were furs, fish, and gold. Settlers came to Alaska in the 1700s and 1800s looking for furs. Good fishing brought many settlers to the state in the 1870s. Gold brought prospectors into the state in the late 1890s.

Currently, the most important natural resource of Alaska is the land itself. Its natural beauty and rich animal and plant life are part of the natural resources. Millions of acres of national parks, preserves, and wilderness cover the land.

Alaska was known for furs, fish, and gold.

Oil is another natural resource. Developed countries depend on oil. There are concerns between people who want to preserve Alaska's wilderness and those who want to develop its oil.

Gold and silver exist in many regions of Alaska. The Panhandle contains nickel, zinc, and lead. Minerals in and around the Gulf of Alaska include mercury, copper, and platinum. Oil, however, will continue to be the most important mining resource for the foreseeable future.

The Trans Alaska Pipeline runs through beautiful areas. Many people worry about oil spills, but others want this important natural resource developed.

Industry

Alaska's largest industries are oil, tourism, and fishing. Timber, mining, and agriculture are also important for the economy.

A sportsman happily shows off his catch—a big salmon.

The Trans Alaska Pipeline takes oil from the far north and sends it to the south side of Alaska. This accounts for the biggest part of the Alaskan economy.

Tourism has grown in Alaska. Ferries and tours give sightseeing trips. More than 1.4 million visitors see Alaska every year.

A cruise ship sails by a glacier.

The seafood industry employs many Alaskans. Fishing is done mostly off the southern coasts. Salmon is the most common catch. Fishing fleets also

A fisherman holds an Alaskan Dungeness crab. These crabs are prized in homes and restaurants for their tastiness.

catch herring, pollack, cod, halibut, crabs, and shrimp.

Alaska contains half the nation's coal reserves. The silver and zinc mines are the nation's largest. Companies mine for gold near Nome. Platinum is mined near the coast of the Bering Sea.

Sports

Alaska has a lot of outdoor recreation. Hunting, fishing, hiking, skiing, snowshoeing, and boating are all important pastimes. Outfitters and boaters help people experience remote parts of Alaska.

Snowshoers under the aurora borealis.

Alaska has two professional sports teams. The Alaska Wild is a football team that plays in the Indoor Football League. The Alaska Aces play in the hockey league known as ECHL. This league prepares players to serve in the National Hockey League.

The state sport is dog mushing. The dogs, often Siberian huskies, pull a sled. Siberian huskies love to pull sleds, and are happy when they are running. Their thick coats keep them warm during the cold. The most famous of the dog mushing races is the Iditarod Trail Sled Dog Race. This race is run in the spring each year.

Alaska's state sport is dog mushing.

Entertainment

Alaska's history is rich with many influences. The art, language, and culture of the many native peoples, once almost lost, is beginning to appear again.

The customs and crafts of Native Alaskans continue to be very important. From hand-made crafts to large totem poles, early Native Alaskans had a variety of skills. These skills are being taught again. For example, in Sitka the Native Alaskans carve totem poles in the traditional way, and teach that skill to others.

A totem pole at Saxman
Totem Park in Ketchikan, Alaska.

Juneau, Anchorage, and other communities have large museums and historical libraries. Music festivals are common, such as the Fairbanks Winter Folk Fest, the Anchorage Folk Festival, the Sitka Summer Music Festival, and the Athabascan Old-Time Fiddling Festival. Fairbanks has an annual month-long ice sculpture contest called the World Ice Art Championships.

A snow sculpture in Barrow

An ice sculpture at the World Ice Art Championships in Fairbanks, Alaska.

Timeline

1725-1728—Vitus Bering explores the area known today as the Bering Strait.

1741—Vitus Bering lands in Alaska. The Russian fur trade begins.

The U.S. flag is raised in Sitka, Alaska, in 1867.

1784—Russians establish the first permanent non-native settlement at Three Saints Bay, Kodiak.

1804—Russians settle at the modern site of Sitka.

1867—The U.S. purchases Alaska from Russia.

1890—Large salmon canneries begin to appear.

1897-1900—The Klondike gold rush.

1916—First bill for Alaska statehood introduced in Congress.

1923—The Alaska Railroad opens for business.

1959—Alaska becomes 49th state in the Union.

1964—Good Friday Earthquake hits with a magnitude of 9.2 on the Richter Scale. It is the largest earthquake ever recorded in North America. It destroys $311 million worth of property in towns near Prince William Sound.

1971—Alaska Native Claims Settlement Act signed into law, returning some ancestral land to Alaskan Natives.

1977—Trans Alaska Pipeline completed from Prudhoe Bay to Valdez.

1989—The Exxon Valdez, a 987-foot (301-m) oil tanker carrying 53 million gallons (201 million liters) of oil runs aground. It spills 11 million gallons (42 million liters) of oil into the pristine Prince William Sound.

2006—Sarah Palin becomes the first woman governor of Alaska.

Glossary

Alaska Native—Any one of the tribes or groups who were native to Alaska before the Europeans came to the area. This includes Inuits, Inuvialuits, Inupiats, Naukans, Yupiks, Yup'iks, Alutiias, Athabascans, Tlingits, and others.

Bering Strait—The small waterway that divides Siberia from Alaska. It was discovered by Vitus Bering in 1728.

Glacier—A large body of ice, formed from melting and refreezing snow, that can slowly spread outward or retreat.

Ice Field—Large fields of ice that flow down a hill or mountain and feed a glacier.

Iditarod—The annual Iditarod Trail Sled Dog Race is a 1,150 mile (1,851 km) race from Anchorage to Nome.

Klondike Gold Rush—A discovery of gold in the Canadian Klondike between 1897 and 1900.

Permafrost—Ground that is frozen for at least two years. Many regions of Alaska have some level of permafrost.

Trans Alaska Pipeline—A pipeline designed to carry oil, built from 1975 to 1977. It starts at the oil deposits in far north Alaska and pipes the oil more than 800 miles (1,287 km) to the port city of Valdez in the south.

Those who live in Alaska find it to be a harsh but beautiful state.

Index